Original title:
The Claws of the Crab

Copyright © 2025 Creative Arts Management OÜ
All rights reserved.

Author: Juliette Kensington
ISBN HARDBACK: 978-1-80587-248-1
ISBN PAPERBACK: 978-1-80587-718-9

## Secrets Encased in Coral

With a twitch and a clack, they dance through the sea,
Thinking they're sly, oh how funny they be!
Hiding their treasures, all shiny and bright,
Yet their secrets leak out, in the moon's silver light.

Crabs in tuxedos, a gala at play,
Wiggling their pincers in such a grand way.
They gossip and giggle, a crusty old crew,
While plotting for snacks that might float into view.

## Crustacean Conundrum

Oh what a puzzle, these critters so bold,
With a waddle so funny, like stories retold.
One claims it can dance, the other just waves,
Yet both are expert at hiding their caves.

They crack jokes by the shore, with shells as their props,
Inventing new games like the best of pals' hops.
And each time they scuttle, they trip on their feet,
Like living comedians on the beach, oh so sweet!

## Of Shells and Secrets

Under the stars, in a tranquil display,
Crustaceans convene for a clam-filled buffet.
With shells on their backs, they join in the fun,
Trading their secrets, all one by one.

Each shell tells a story, a riddle, a laugh,
Mixed with the waves, it's their chosen craft.
Cracking their jokes like a nut in the sand,
Pretending they're kings of this wat'ry land.

## In the Grip of the Tides

When the tides start to dance, they wobble and sway,
These crusty companions just want to play.
With a clumsy embrace, they tumble and spin,
Trying their best to keep balance and grin.

In the grip of the tide, they're both nimble and sly,
Chasing each other with a wink and a sigh.
And if one gets stuck in a pile of wet sand,
The others will giggle, and give them a hand.

## Grasping at Shadows

Beneath the sun, they scuttle and play,
With tiny pincers that dance all day.
They pinch at the air, but mostly at sand,
Chasing their dreams, but none were quite planned.

In shadows they lurk, with mischief so bright,
Their silly antics are quite a sight.
With no sense of timing, they stumble and trip,
All while pretending they're kings of the grip.

## Moonlit Tides and Hardened Armor

Under the moon, they strike such a pose,
In shiny armor, with curious toes.
They march in a line, so awkward and bold,
Claiming each grain of sand like it's gold.

A dance of the shells, a slap and a sway,
Tickled by waves that come in to play.
They're ready for battle, but what's there to fight?
Just seagulls above and stars shining bright!

## A Dance on the Shoreline

On the shoreline they gather, all ruff and no fluff,
With a rhythm that's quirky, a style that's tough.
They wiggle and wriggle in a silly display,
Dancing to tunes only they can convey.

With each little shuffle, they chance turning tails,
As waves roll in gently, sharing their tales.
They twirl and they tumble, it's quite the charade,
In the sandy spotlight, a spectacle made.

## Whispering Waves of the Ocean's Edge

At the water's edge, a chatty parade,
Each silent whisper hides a grand charade.
They speak in soft nudges, and pinch with a flair,
While giggling with seashells, they've no time to care.

As the tide rises up, they scatter in fright,
No grandiose plans, just a fun silly sight.
With laughter they blend, as the ocean's their friend,
Making waves with each pinch, till the last round extends.

## A Guardian's Secret Night

By moonlight danced a scaly knight,
With shells and armor shining bright.
He sneaked away from beachside cheer,
For secret snacks and fashion near.

With prawn and fries tucked in his shell,
He laughed and twirled; all was well.
A crab in splendor, not a care,
He munched with flair, a gourmet rare.

## Clutching Moments Cast Away

With pincers poised for mischief's call,
He pinches friends, he pinches all.
"A hug!" he says, while they all scream,
His grip's a thrill, a twisty dream.

By sandcastles, his jokes emerge,
He claims the crown, a regal surge.
But slips and tumbles send him flying,
A splat on sand, the laughter's vying.

## Beneath the Armor's Heart

A crab with secrets, what a sight,
With heart so big, but prone to fright.
His armor strong, but soft within,
He blushes bright, a silly grin.

He dreams of dance beneath the tide,
With jellyfish, he'll turn and glide.
Yet when they twirl, he trips and flops,
His fancy shoes? Just rubber tops.

## The Sea's Gritty Remnants

Upon the shore, he digs for loot.
Treasure found? Just more sea fruit!
A shiny shell? A snack? Oh dear!
He munches right, forgetting fear.

But as he chomps on salty goo,
He finds a crab hat: oh what a coup!
His friends all cheer, they join the fun,
A crab parade beneath the sun.

## Salted Armor and Grit

In the sand they scuttle fast,
With shells that shine, none can outlast.
A dance of joy, they twist and spin,
Who knew such fun could come from fin?

They wave their arms, oh what a sight,
To pinch a toe, is pure delight!
With salty armor strong and bright,
They jest and play, through day and night.

## A Journey Through Rocky Refuges

Beneath the rocks, they plot and scheme,
With cheeky grins, they chase a dream.
A leap, a pop, a splash in tide,
Their laughter echoing, far and wide.

In little nooks, they hide and peek,
With tiny claws, they play hide and seek.
A game of tag, so swift and spry,
Who knew such fun would swim nearby?

## Reflections under the Sea's Glimmer

In shallow pools, they strike a pose,
With shiny shells, and funny toes.
Each ripple sparkles with their cheer,
What a sight, oh dear, oh dear!

They mirror dances of the waves,
With sideway shuffles, and funny raves.
A whimsical ballet, they display,
Who knew the sea could be this playful way?

## The Trade Winds and Their Keepers

As breezes blow, they chase the fun,
On sunny shores, beneath the sun.
With little pirouettes in the sand,
These tiny jesters, oh how they stand!

When winds do change, they scurry fast,
A harmless game, a joyous cast.
With giggles shared upon the shore,
They play and laugh forevermore.

## **Emblems of Coastal Life**

On the sandy shore they dance,
With sideways steps, a funny prance.
Doesn't care if you may stare,
Just a pinch of salty flair.

Their little pincers, oh so bold,
Hold secrets that are yet untold.
In a shell, they're undercover,
Witty jests and tales of blubber.

With sunhats made of driftwood fine,
They gossip over sips of brine.
A beachside party, what a scene,
Laughter mixed with seaweed green.

But should you step upon their toes,
Watch out for crabbing comic woes!
A sideways chase across the sand,
Their quick retreat, a funny band.

## An Odyssey of the Currents

Across the foam, they gallivant,
Riding waves with youthful slant.
A twist and turn, they duck and dive,
Silly tricks help them survive.

With matching shells in varied hues,
They flaunt their style while singing blues.
They challenge fish with silly bets,
The ocean floor fills up with debts.

A whirlpool spins, they lose their place,
It's a whirlwind crabby race!
With laughter echoing through the sea,
These crustaceans know how to be free.

But beware the otters swimming by,
With quick paws, they'll surely try,
To steal the best in all their stock,
Leaving crabs to dance and mock.

## Heartbeats of the Glistening Tide

When dusk arrives, they come alive,
With jokes and jabs, they take a dive.
The moon above, a gleeful grin,
As comrades spark a joke or spin.

In shallow pools where secrets bloom,
They plot a rise and make some room.
With laughter bubbling like the sea,
They craft a riddle, goofy spree.

One crab slips on a seaweed vine,
A clumsy twirl, a funny line.
While others laugh and wiggle tight,
Their nightly mischief feels just right.

As tides come in to wash the shore,
Their giggles echo, forevermore.
These heartbeats in the glimmering tide,
Remind us all to take the ride.

## The Unseen Conversations at Dusk

As light fades low, they gather near,
With chit and chat that draws a cheer.
In whispers soft, they craft a plot,
A secret dance, begun on the spot.

Two friends debate the way to roam,
With spicy tales of their underwater home.
One speaks of pearls, the other laughs,
As they create their crafty gaffs.

Watch for shadows as they engage,
These snappy fellas on the stage.
With humor high and wits so sly,
They jest together, oh me, oh my!

Yet danger lurks with every wave,
They hide their jokes, so quick and brave.
But if you listen, you might just hear,
Their funny tales of yesteryear.

## Crimson Grip of the Tides

In the sand, a pinch of fun,
A little critter on the run.
With bulging eyes, it scuttles fast,
Its sideways dance, a comical blast.

It waved a claw, an awkward show,
Chasing friends in a clumsy flow.
With every lurch, laughter erupts,
As it leaps over waves, then abruptly flops.

The beachgoers laugh, pointing and grin,
At its quirky moves, like a spin on a pin.
With every tick of salty spray,
That little gaffer steals the day!

When stars come out and the sun goes down,
The king of the rocks wears a goofy crown.
In the moonlight's glow, its shadow gleams,
Waving goodbye to our sandy dreams.

## **Secrets Beneath the Shell**

Underneath the waves so blue,
Dwells a fellow, out of view.
With secrets held in each small shell,
It plots a laugh; oh, can you tell?

As it peeks out with curious flair,
You'd think it's plotting a fancy affair.
Instead, it slips, with a splash and a flop,
Leaving us giggling, as it starts to hop.

Oh, the stories that little one knows,
Of sunken ships and seaweed grows.
With a wink and a wiggle, it spins around,
A master of mischief, where laughs abound.

When it finally retreats to the coast,
We toast to the critter we love the most.
For every bob and giggle it shares,
Brings joy to the sea and all who dares!

**Shadows of the Rocky Shore**

On the rocks, a shadow flits,
With a sideways swagger and playful wits.
It's a chubby feller, smiling wide,
As it dusts off sand from its side.

With a wink and squint, it peers at me,
Challenging the waves, so wild and free.
As crabs can do, it flips and rolls,
Turning beach days into comedy strolls.

The barnacles cheer, they're quite the crowd,
Every tiny move, they declare it proud.
While people laugh at the silly show,
It clinks its claws, putting on a glow.

When the tide pulls back, and shadows grow,
That spirited creature steals the show.
With its laughter echoing off the land,
It leaves us grinning, just as it planned.

## Embrace of the Sea's Sentinel

Not a warrior, but a silly friend,
With claws that wave like they'll throw and bend.
Perched on a rock with a goofy stance,
It's ready to battle in a clumsy dance.

Onlookers chuckle, what a sight to see,
Its antics unfold so clumsily free.
A silly moment on the shoreline spins,
Where the guardian winks with toothy grins.

It skitters left and then jumps right,
With each little bound, it stars in the light.
As it tussles with seaweed, oh what a roar,
Making the best of life on the shore.

When tides rumble back with playful might,
This awkward sentinel takes flight.
Till the sun dips low in twilight's glow,
We cheer for the humor it puts on show.

## Dance of the Prickly Guardian

Beneath the moon, they prance around,
Tiny soldiers, never making a sound.
With their pincers raised, they boast and tease,
Shuffling sideways, like a crafty breeze.

With a wiggle and a jiggle, they steal the show,
Creeping on the sand, moving to and fro.
Funny little dancers with armor so tight,
In their crooked ballet, they bring sheer delight.

Each wave a partner, pulling them near,
Holding them close, whispering in cheer.
A crabby caper beneath starlit skies,
Their laughter echoes as they shimmy and rise.

## The Silent Watcher of the Shoreline

Upon the rocks, a lookout stands tall,
Still as a statue, you'd think it a wall.
With eyes like marbles, they're ever so sly,
Waiting for snacks as the tide rolls by.

With a pinch and a snap, they plot their raid,
Mischievous glances, a secret brigade.
Their humor's subtle, like grains of sand,
Chortling silently at their own crafty plan.

They skitter and scatter, oh what a sight,
A rascal parade, dancing under moonlight.
With claws that are ready, they play their part,
The silent jokers of the ocean's heart.

## Beneath the Waves' Guardianship

In the deep, where the currents play,
Silly creatures hold court every day.
With shells on their backs and twinkling eyes,
Guardians of giggles, beneath sunlit skies.

They hide in the rocks, peeking with glee,
Wondering what kind of snacks they might see.
A noodle of seaweed, or maybe a chip,
Every morsel is cause for a crabby trip.

Yet taking a stroll, they frolic in air,
Waving their claws without a care.
With every shuffle, a giggle ensues,
Who knew crustaceans could dance with such moves?

**Echoes from the Sand**

Tales of the beach travel far and near,
Whispers of fun that we all hold dear.
Beneath the surface, they plot and they scheme,
Little cheeky legends, living the dream.

With curls of laughter coating the shore,
Gossiping softly, they long for more.
Chubby little critters, with joy they expand,
Making merry mischief in a golden land.

As they play tag with the shimmering foam,
They dance to the rhythm, feeling at home.
In the echoes of sand, their giggles resound,
Life under the sun, in silliness found.

## A Fisherman's Lament

Oh, I dropped my bait in the sea,
That sneaky crab took it from me.
With pincers sharp and a cheeky grin,
He danced away, my chances thin.

I cast my line with hope and care,
But crabs are clever, I must beware.
They're not fish, but they join the show,
In this grand ocean, they're the stars, you know.

I told my mates a tale too grand,
About that crab who stole my hand.
They laughed so hard, they nearly cried,
While I just pouted and sighed aside.

Yet here's the truth, it's kind of swell,
To see them scuttle, don't you tell.
For every catch lost on this night,
Folly's richer with laughter's light.

## Scuttling Across Fading Light

In shadows deep, they make their rush,
Those little critters, a frantic hush.
With sideways steps and sneaky sneers,
They claim the beach, unending cheers.

I chased them down with bucket wide,
But they were quick, they caught the tide.
Like tiny prancers, all in a row,
They dashed away, what a sly show!

A flash of shells, they dashed to flee,
Who knew they'd win this game with glee?
I stood alone with only sand,
Tipped my hat to their crafty hand.

At dusk, they laugh, at least, it seems,
In their scuttling race towards night's dreams.
While I just ponder what could be,
If I could catch just one, oh me!

## The Ocean's Gnarled Embrace

The waves roll in with mischief played,
But crabs don't care, they've got it made.
With armor tough and little quirks,
They rule the shore, grinning with smirks.

I set my trap with pies and cheese,
Those wily folks just dance with ease.
I blinked, and there went my fine bait,
Leaving me stuck with just my fate.

Each time I think I've got the knack,
They scuttle forth, my plans all whack.
How do they know? It's quite absurd,
They've surely formed a secret herd.

But here's the fun, despite my woes,
Their laughter echoes as the tide slows.
So I'll bring treats, come what may,
For every crab deserves some play!

## Secrets of the Marin Twilight

As night falls soft on the sandy floor,
Crabs come alive, all wanting more.
In the twilight, their shadows creep,
With playful antics that make me leap.

I watch in awe, what a strange sight,
Those little dancers, full of delight.
With sideways moves and crafty schemes,
They twist and turn in my wild dreams.

I'll never catch them, that much is clear,
They've mastered the art, there's nothing to fear.
Yet every evening, I find pure joy,
In their cheeky ways, they're my favorite ploy.

So here's to the twilight, the fun won't fade,
For every crab's tail, a story's made.
In laughter and folly, we all unite,
Salted with joy in the cool nightlight.

## Moonlit Mirage of Sharp Edges

In the moonlight they plot, so bold,
With pincers that glint like gold.
They dance on the shore, quite a sight,
In a ballet of pinch and quite the fright.

Sandy partners they prance with glee,
Tap-dancing like they own the sea.
For a snack, they crave a juicy fry,
While dodging the waves and the gulls that fly.

Beneath the surface, they whisper tales,
Of bold adventures and fanciful gales.
They chuckle and snicker, quite the ruse,
"Watch out for toes, they're here to amuse!"

So, here's to the creatures with shells so tough,
Life's a banquet; they can't get enough.
With each little pinch is a giggle and grin,
In this ocean of mischief, let the fun begin!

## Timeless Steps of the Salty Abyss.

At twilight they shuffle, with nary a care,
Sideways they sashay, a nautical flair.
In the salty abyss, they're waltzing with pride,
Their dance floor is wet; on the tide they glide.

With a snap and a crack, they clap in delight,
While munching on snacks in the cool moonlight.
They chitter and chatter, oh what a scene,
Each step seems a stunt from a wacky dream.

A whiskered delight, they strut and they pose,
In shells like fine armor, they strike a grand rose.
They tickle the sand and wiggle about,
Who knew crustaceans could dance with such clout?

Yes, under the stars, they've mastered the art,
Of silly jazz moves that warm the heart.
A round of applause for this clamorous crew,
Taking wobbly steps in a wavy debut!

## Pinchers of Fate

With pincers a-twitch, they plan their next feast,
A glorious chase, to say the least.
Each snap brings a cheer, like a toast in the air,
To the bounty of snacks that float without care.

They scuttle and scoot, in a jolly little race,
With moves like a ninja, they quicken the pace.
"Ahoy, there's a chip!" one says with a grin,
And off they all bolt for a crispy win.

Legs like little springs, they hop on the sand,
Chasing each morsel, a whimsical band.
"Who knew we could have such fun in the night?"
They laugh in the dark, their joy pure delight.

Oh, take heed of their antics and clever charades,
For a simple snack leads to wild escapades.
Life's full of surprises, just wait and you'll see,
As they dance in the moonlight, so joyful and free!

## Secrets Beneath the Shell

Beneath the hard shell lies laughter and glee,
A treasure of giggles, just wait and see.
They whisper sweet secrets to each passing wave,
With antics and pranks, they're ever so brave.

At dawn, they'll emerge with tales to impart,
Of mischief and fun, with a pinch of smart.
"Did you see that fellow who lost his way?
He stumbled and tumbled, what a display!"

In the soft sandy beds, they host a grand soirée,
With seaweed confetti for a fancy buffet.
Bobbing about, in a clam shell they feast,
As laughter erupts, they find joy at least!

So, raise a small cheer for the silly and spry,
For life in the ocean is no reason to sigh.
Each nibble and nudge brings moments of fun,
In the realm of the sea, laughter's never done!

## Clutching Narratives of the Shore

On sandy beaches, tales unfold,
A crab with stories, brave and bold.
It struts around with a snap and a pinch,
While seagulls watch, they scoff and flinch.

With sidesteps quirky, a comical dance,
Each move a jest, a daring prance.
The tide rolls in, a wave of cheer,
The silly crab waves, "Come join me here!"

Beneath bright skies, it takes a bet,
A race with shells, a new vignette.
Its tiny friends cheer on the side,
As laughter mingles with the tide.

So if you see a shell-bound chap,
Wink and chuckle, give him a clap.
For every crab with a story to share,
Sprinkles of joy dance in the air.

## Navigating the Underworld

In the depths, a sneaky tale,
A crafty creature on its trail.
With beady eyes and a jabby claw,
It waves hello with an awkward draw.

Through seaweed forests, it scuttles around,
A little mischief is always found.
Dodging fish and a playful stingray,
It grins wide, as if to say—

"I'm on a quest for treasures bright,
A shiny shell, a pearl of light!"
It trips on rocks with a gleeful laugh,
And claims the sea as its photograph.

With every twist, the journey's bold,
In ocean's depths, adventures unfold.
This crusty character, with charm and glee,
Reminds us laughter is the key!

## Echoes of a Hidden Kingdom

In a kingdom beneath the waves,
Lives a ruler with heaps of knaves.
With a crown of shells, it struts so proud,
Announcing its rule, it laughs out loud.

Cracking jokes with a bubbly cheer,
Its loyal minions gather near.
Each witty pun and silly jest,
Brings joy to all and never rests.

Like royalty, it rules the floor,
With flipping antics on the shore.
It hoards laughter like a treasure chest,
While sunbeams glint, they feel so blessed.

So come and bask where the fun beams bright,
As echoes of laughter fill the night.
In this hidden kingdom, dive and play,
For jesters thrive where the seaweed sway.

## The Silent Sentinels of the Bay

On rocky ledges, a watchful band,
Silent sentinels, all unplanned.
With claws like swords and shells like shields,
They guard the secrets of ocean fields.

Their eyes survey the watery brine,
In perfect stillness, they feel divine.
Yet when a wave sends splashes high,
They leap in joy, beneath the sky.

With raucous giggles, they play all day,
A dance of silliness as they sway.
Though stoic at first, they can't resist,
The urge to play in a wet twist.

They're clever little guardians, it's true,
With every wave, they wax anew.
So cherish those sillies by the bay,
For laughter is never far away.

## Legends of Lifeguard Shores

On sandy shores where sunbathers sprawl,
A crab in shades calls out, "Come, one and all!"
With tiny waves, he mimics life guard's stance,
"Don't swim too far, this isn't your dance!"

He sidesteps swiftly, his style so unique,
While tourists chuckle, 'He's the one we seek!'
With a whistle made of seashells, he trains,
Exposing all our sunburns and our pains!

Beneath the umbrella, he takes a bold break,
Snacking on fries, claiming it's for his sake.
While children giggle and try to outrun,
This crustacean lifeguard—oh, he's so fun!

So if you're swimming and hear a strange sound,
It might be the crab, paddling around!
He'll save your sunscreen, with a flick of his claw,
Remember the legend, the shores' funny law!

## **The Shells Beneath the Storm**

Beneath the waves, where secrets reside,
A crab cracks jokes with the currents' slide.
While shells dance wildly in a salty ballet,
He rolls his eyes at the seagulls' foray.

"Oh dear," he quips, "the storm's come to play,
Why does it always pick this beach day?"
He juggles with shells, a true circus act,
His antics unfurl like the ocean's own pact.

With buddies all hollering, "Let's build a fort!"
They hide from the squalls in a clam-shell resort.
"Hey, be careful!" he shouts, "that's my last chip!
Leave room for the dip; we're planning a trip!"

As thunder rolls in, they laugh and dive deep,
Making a game of the storm's angry sweep.
From seaweed crowns to camaraderie grand,
These undersea jokers, the heart of the sand!

## Underwater Chronicles

In the depths where fish sing and coral glows bright,
A crab in a tuxedo looks quite out of sight.
With a top hat that wobbles, he dances a jig,
Shooting the currents like a shimmering twig.

"Welcome, my friends, to my underwater show,
With guests from the ocean, come gather and glow!"
As squids play the drums, and eels take the mic,
He steals the spotlight, quite the daring tyke.

Between seaweed curtains and bubbles that pop,
This crusty performer just can't seem to stop.
"I'll tell you a story, it's filled with a twist,
About fish who misbehave and sunken treasure missed!"

As laughter erupts from the gathered seahorse,
They celebrate life in a watery course.
So if you duck down and hear jokes filled with glee,
Know the crab's just performing beneath the sea!

## The Tempest's Grip

When clouds roll in, and the rain starts to pour,
The crab puts on his raincoat, ready to score.
With a flick and a flail, he splashes about,
Making waves of laughter, without any doubt.

"Grab your umbrellas!" he shouts with a grin,
"Let's dance to the rhythm, let the fun begin!"
As puddles form pools, he leaps with a cheer,
"The storm can't catch us, it's just for a year!"

With his crabby pals doing the crabcake twist,
They twirl and they whirl, oh, no way to resist!
"Watch out for the thunder!" he jokes, quite absurd,
"I'm the crab of the storm; haven't you heard?"

So when tempestuous storms fill the skies,
Just think of the crab and his laughter that flies.
With whimsy and wit, he'll always uplift,
In every downpour, he's a fanciful gift!

## Echoes of a Twelve-Legged Legend

In a tide pool, a crustacean pranced,
With a dance that left all critters entranced.
He strutted and hopped, clicking his claws,
Claiming the shore as he broke all the laws.

He wore a top hat made of old seaweed,
Challenging fish to a dance-off with speed.
When waved goodbye, he gave quite a show,
Jiving like no one could catch him, oh no!

With each little jig, he scattered his foes,
As seagulls above watched with curious woes.
"Don't pinch me!" cried a clam with a grin,
As the crusty dude danced, a life full of sin.

So here's to the legend, the twelve-legged king,
Hip-hop on the beach, oh what joy he brings!
With laughter and joy, let the seaweed sway,
For the crustacean dancer. Hip-hip-hooray!

## An Offering on the Tidal Edge

At the water's edge, gifts laid out,
Mollusks and shells, with giggles about.
A crab had a plan with some slimy bait,
To charm all the fish, it was never too late.

"Come taste my feast!" he cried with great flair,
But fish rolled their eyes, said they didn't care.
Yet he danced in circles, a most cunning sight,
A sea buffet act, oh, what pure delight!

With kelp as his crown, he strutted like mad,
As crabs all around thought, "This dance isn't bad!"
Krill came along, they giggled and cheered,
While the fish just swam away, totally weirded.

So tides keep on turning, and laughter flows free,
With offerings made from crustacean glee.
While fish stay aloof, and crabs misbehave,
It's laughter and joy that the surf's gonna crave!

## Harmony Amidst the Exoskeleton

In the shallow waters, a band played loud,
A crusty musician, he drew quite a crowd.
With maracas of shells and a slippery beat,
He made all the minnows get up on their feet.

Snapping his pincers to keep the time right,
He brought in the waves for a wild dance fight.
With laughter and bubbles, they twirled in the spray,
As fish in a frenzy just tried to get away.

The seagulls all cawed, with feathers a-blur,
"We're crabs of great talent, come join the furor!"
So all around them, the rhythm did swell,
With laughter and joy, their laughter would tell.

From the depths of the ocean to sandy shorelines,
The beat of the crab made a symphony fine.
In harmony's glow, they danced through their shells,
In seaweed and laughter, where fun always dwells!

## **Castaway's Reverie**

Upon a small rock, a boulder of dreams,
Sat a lonely crab with thoughts full of schemes.
He longed for adventure, to dance and to play,
While the tide washed in all his worries away.

He fancied a ship, with sails of sea foam,
Where hermit crabs gather, far away from home.
As he daydreamed on, he made quite the scene,
Imagining treasure and a pirate's cuisine.

But, alas, the calls of a seagull nearby,
Woke the crustacean right out of the sky.
"Hey crab, dreamer, why not join my crew?"
While he clicked his pincers, the thoughts only grew.

So with a gleeful grin, he leapt off the rock,
Embracing the chance to dance 'round the dock.
In a world full of laughter, where dreams find a way,
Our crustaceous hero still lives for today!

## Traces in the Sand

Little crabs scuttle about,
With sideways steps, they dance and shout.
They leave behind marks in the sand,
As if drawing a map, so unplanned.

With tiny pincers waving high,
They seem to flirt with the sky.
A creature so bold, yet so shy,
In their little world, they fly by!

Each wave that crashes, they cheer with glee,
In the grains of sand, they all agree.
It's a game of hide and seek, quite grand,
In a vast beach theater, it's their land.

And when the sunset starts to glow,
They wave goodbye, then quickly go.
Leaving traces, oh-so-funny,
In a world that's warm and sunny!

## A Shell's Memories

The shells tell tales of days gone by,
Adventures beneath a pastel sky.
One once boasted it was a king,
But life as a shell's not quite that thing.

Worn smooth by tides, but with pride,
It laughs at the fish that try to hide.
"Once I had a friend," it would boast,
"A seagull who thought it could coast!"

Ears to the shore, where waves collide,
The shell still dreams of its wild ride.
Imagination in the foam,
Allows it to travel far from home.

So next time you spot one on the strand,
Remember the jokes in the silent sand.
A little humor held inside,
In every shell where dreams abide.

## Footprints of Tenacity

In the wet sand, traces abound,
Miniature footprints all around.
Each little step is brave and bold,
A story of triumph silently told.

A battle with waves, they never tire,
Dodging splashes like a live wire.
With hearts so big in tiny frames,
These little marchers, oh, what names!

They dance with the tide, side to side,
Playing tag while the gulls glide.
With every wave that tries to erase,
They leave tiny tracks that hold their trace.

So if you see them on your way,
Don't shoo them off and make them sway.
For life is fun when you explore,
The footprints of tenacity—forever more!

## **Resilience Amidst Waves**

Beneath the surf, a comedy spree,
Tiny warriors of the sea.
With every wave, they flip and flop,
Yet laugh it off and never stop.

They dig and dart, without a care,
Defying physics, they leap through air.
With a wink and smile, they claim their throne,
In a watery realm that's all their own!

With shells for shields and minds so keen,
They navigate chaos like a dream.
In a world of splash, they raise their claws,
To conquer setbacks with little flaws.

So here's to the ones who brave the sea,
Teaching us how to be carefree.
In the face of tides, they don't behave,
Resilience like theirs? Now that's being brave!

## Signposts of Summer's End

In the sand, a little pincher,
Dancing like a tiny flincher,
With its shell all shiny bright,
Laughing under the moonlight.

Jumps and prances with a flair,
Cracks a smile, doesn't seem to care,
Waves its pincers, proud as can be,
As goofy as a crab can see.

Seagulls cackle from above,
While our friend just looks for love,
Chasing shells like they're a prize,
A crustacean with silly eyes.

As autumn breezes start to stir,
This beach buddy turns to blur,
To find a cozy spot to hide,
And wait for winter's chilly tide.

## Beacons in the Seafoam

In the foam, a prankster lurks,
With a stance that surely smirks,
Pincers up, it's ready to play,
Surprising beachgoers in a splashy way.

Bouncing sideways, what a sight!
In and out, it's full of fright,
Pretends to chase, oh so spry,
While clam diggers pass it by.

The ocean giggles, waves roll high,
While our hero waves goodbye,
With every drift, a giggling shout,
Who knew the sea could be so sprout?

As the sun dips low in the sky,
Our comical friend waves its bye,
But don't fret, it'll return soon.
With laughter echoing in the dunes.

## Unfurling of the Ocean's Script

Written in the shifting sand,
A funny tale by nature's hand,
With antics fit for any stage,
A crusty star, a pinch of rage.

As tides unfold the ocean's book,
A little crab gives a funny look,
With skittering feet on its crazy quest,
It steals the scene with its little jest.

A dash here and a dash there,
Who knew a crab could dance with flair?
Its glossy shell in the sunlit glow,
With a wink and twirl, it steals the show.

But as the twilight starts to beam,
This comic sea star starts to dream,
Of warmer days to come anew,
And swaying to its favorite tune.

## Metamorphosis of the Riverbed

On the riverbed, amidst the muck,
A wily crab is in good luck,
Climbing rocks with a cheeky grin,
Ready for the games to begin!

It sidesteps with a quirky style,
Every move brings a goofy smile,
Snapping at fish, oh what a show,
While ducklings quack as they swim below.

With each ripple, it plays its part,
In the river's quirky art,
A creature that knows how to jest,
Turning the mundane into a fest!

As shadows lengthen, it bows down low,
To the river creatures in a row,
With tales of laughter to share around,
What a delight in the muddy ground!

## The Guardian of the Sand

In armor shell and mighty grip,
A sentinel with a sideways trip.
It rules the beach with regal flare,
Twirling grains without a care.

With pinchers ready for a snack,
It wanders forth to keep the track.
While sunbathers stare and start to grin,
The little guard just tucks it in.

It shuffles, dances, digs a hole,
With sand adorned, it is a soul.
But watch your toes, oh silly mate,
For reign of claws can never wait.

A laugh erupts, a playful cheer,
As it prances to a tune we hear.
With tiny feet, it takes a stand,
We salute you, guardian of the sand!

## Scuttling Through Time

In a world where time stands still,
It marches on with utmost skill.
Scuttling hard with zestful pride,
A tiny time lord with nothing to hide.

Through grains of sand, it weaves a tale,
Of lost flip-flops and shrimp cocktail.
With laughter echoing in the breeze,
A crustacean chasing memories with ease.

Tick tock, the hours do grow,
Yet this crafty thing puts on a show.
With a twirl and a quick little spin,
It covers up its cheeky grin.

So when you see it racing past,
Know that joy is not meant to last.
Just smile and let your worries go,
As it scuttles on, putting on its show.

## Embrace of Salt and Salinity

In tidal pools, where wonders play,
A zesty beast brightens the day.
With salty hugs and briny cheer,
It scuttles forth, drawing near.

With wiry limbs and quirks galore,
It boogies like it's hit the floor.
A crabby dance of joy and jest,
In waves of salt, it feels the best.

Embraced by sea's warm, foamy kiss,
It churns through life, who could resist?
With every jig, it tells a tale,
No need for roads, it'll never fail.

So lift a shell to the sand-filled throne,
Where humor reigns, and crabs feel at home.
Let's laugh together, share this spree,
With a pinch and a wink, how fun it can be!

## Echoes from the Ocean's Depths

From ocean's heart, the laughter flows,
A crustacean tale that no one knows.
With joyous booms from under the sea,
It tickles fins in playful glee.

It sends out echoes that bounce and sway,
As creatures join in silly play.
A choir of laughs, a bubbly tune,
In watery realms, they dance till noon.

Flippers flapping, a wave of delight,
Bringing joy from morning to night.
With every chuckle, the waves do tease,
Life's a party where all are pleased.

So dive right in, let laughter be bold,
In the dance of the deep, stories unfold.
With echoes ringing, come join the fun,
In a realm where the ocean is never done!

## Tidal Secrets and Hidden Depths

In the shallow waves, they dance and prance,
With sideways steps, they take a chance.
Lobster and shrimp, oh what a sight,
Holiday feasts, we munch with delight.

They pinch and poke, a playful brawl,
With tiny claws, they tackle it all.
In tides that swirl, adventures begin,
Dressed in armor, they laugh with a grin.

Seeking treasures where seaweed sways,
Building castles in playful displays.
Beneath the sun, they giggle and play,
Chasing their shadows, all through the day.

When crabs collide, it's a comical show,
As they scuttle fast, pretending to blow.
With each little bump, they boast and boast,
In the salty sea, it's the crustaceans' roast.

## Specters of Saltwater Dreams

Under the moonlight, they roam and glide,
With shells that shimmer, they set the tide.
From sandy burrows, they peek with glee,
Whispering secrets of the deep blue sea.

With moonlit jests, they shimmy and sway,
An underwater dance, so bright and gay.
A crab with style, jivin' to the beat,
Crusty old barnacles join in for a treat.

They brag of size, such an epic tale,
Claiming the throne of the ocean trail.
But when the tide turns, they run in fright,
Back to their homes, they flee from the night.

These husky fellows, with eyes so wide,
Do the side-step shuffle, with nothing to hide.
In the frothy surf, they plot and scheme,
Crafting their legends in a saltwater dream.

## Crustacean Tales

Gather round, friends, for a story so bold,
Of clappy clawed critters, all salty and old.
With a pinch and a poke, they chase the day,
In a kingdom of sand where they laugh and play.

A crab once claimed he was king of the sea,
With a crown made of shells, as proud as can be.
But the fish just giggled and swam out of reach,
Saying, "With those tiny claws, you're just out of peach!"

They strut on the shore in their quirky attire,
Shells polished bright, they never tire.
With every sidestep, they wiggle and glide,
In the world of crustaceans, they take full pride.

At twilight's close, they're still on the go,
Searching for snacks that they love to bestow.
With laughter and games, they fill up their plates,
In the banquet of tides, where fun never abates.

## Beneath the Tidal Veil

In the frothy surf, they crawl and crawl,
With goofy grins, they answer the call.
Jiggle and wiggle, they shimmy so bright,
Beneath the waves, they bring pure delight.

With tiny antennas that twitch and flare,
They play hide and seek in the cool ocean air.
But when the tide turns, it's a mad little dash,
As crabs scuttle sideways in a tidal splash.

They trade little tales of the biggest catch,
While polishing shells that are hard to match.
Each night is a carnival under the sea,
Where the laughter echoes from crab to sea flea.

So lift up your flagons, let's toast to the crew,
The crusty companions in the waves so blue.
Together they twirl, a funny parade,
In the briny deep where the memories are made.

## Treasure in the Tidepools

In rocky hollows, treasures hide,
Anemones dance, and sea stars glide.
Crustaceans scuttle, with pinchers raised,
In this watery world, the playful praised.

Glimmers of gold under seaweed sway,
Who knew a hermit could laugh and play?
With shells for homes, they find their place,
In tiny kingdoms, the race for space.

Each wave a giggle, every splash a jest,
Surfing the bubbles, the critters rest.
Barnacles cling, what a sticky style,
Life under the sea has its own weird smile.

So join the fun in this salty spree,
Where every crab holds a comedy key.
In pools of wonder, hilarity blooms,
A treasure trove of ocean's costumes.

## Born of the Roiling Deep

From depths unknown, with a cheeky flair,
A creature emerges, with a mischievous stare.
Clanging a shell like a make-believe drum,
The mariner laughs, oh we're in for some fun!

Tentacles wave in a dance of delight,
A ballet of fish in the moon's silver light.
In swirling currents, the madness does reign,
With laughter and bubbles, all joy in the rain.

This ocean giggle, a riotous song,
A chorus of gurgles, it won't be long.
With jester fish flashing, bright as a rhyme,
They wink and they twirl, to the rhythm of time.

So come take a dive, in waters so steep,
Where humor abounds, we'll roar with the deep.
The waves, they are playful, a jest in the brine,
Born of deep laughter, oh what a divine!

## The Singularity of the Seabed

Down below, where the light plays hide,
Creatures converse in a bubbly tide.
A crab with a monocle, wise yet absurd,
Claims he knows secrets, though seldom is heard.

Starfish declare a contest divine,
To see who can hold the best pose in line.
With a twist and a turn, they all seem to freeze,
Oh snap! They're a sight, catching oceanic breeze.

The octopus juggles with grace, oh what glee!
With a whirl and a whirl, it's a comedy spree.
Each bubble that bursts brings a snicker nearby,
As laughter erupts, from the salt and the sky.

So smile with the currents, let loose and abide,
In the wondrous chasm, where the goofballs reside.
For in this abyss, the hilarity's deep,
Swirling gently like dreams, into the ocean we leap.

## Interlude with the Ocean's Keepers

Gather 'round, all ye sea-bound friends,
A meeting so fine, where laughter transcends.
The crabs wear top hats, the fish in tuxedos,
An underwater gala, with oddities in rows.

"Shall we sing a tune?" the dolphin does quip,
While seaweed sways with the rhythm and flip.
"Here's to our kingdom!" the clam starts to cheer,
While bubbles burst forth, spreading joy far and near.

With wit as their armor, they sprout repartee,
In this grand assembly, so wily and free.
The squid's crackling jokes cause the waves to erupt,
As the audience roars, giggles often interrupt.

So join in the fun, in this splashing parade,
Where every creature is both funny and laid.
An interlude splendid, beneath ocean blue,
Where laughter's the treasure, just waiting for you!

## Armor of the Abyss

In the depths where crabs do stare,
They flaunt their armor, quite the affair.
With pinchers clacking, they dance with glee,
Who knew the sea had such a spree?

These critters strut in marine delight,
In colors bright, oh what a sight!
Their shells like shields, they twist and spin,
Making the ocean a laugh-filled din.

With sideways shuffles and a wink of an eye,
They'll challenge the fish, but oh my oh my!
"Try to catch me!" they seem to say,
As they scuttle fast, getting away.

In the underwater realm so vast and grand,
Some creatures wonder if they're really just planned.
Crabs chuckle softly, "Life's a big show!"
"In our shiny armor, we steal the glow!"

## **Dance of the Coastal Guardians**


Upon the rocks, they take their stance,
With lively moves, they start to prance.
The guardians of shore, in joyous mood,
Making beachgoers feel quite crude.

They twirl and twist, oh what a sight!
With sideways grooves, they own the night.
Beware the pinch, but heed the show,
As they grace the waves with a crabby glow.

Shells gleaming bright under the sun,
Dancing like fools, oh what fun!
With laughter bubbling from ocean's soul,
These crustaceans know how to roll!

From beach to tide, they claim the throne,
In this coastal ball, they're never alone.
With a flip and a snap, their spirits rise,
The dance of guardians – oh how it flies!

## Whispers of the Nautical Night

Under the moon, the waves do sigh,
As crabs come out to croon and pry.
They whisper secrets to the tide,
In a comical way, they roam with pride.

With eyes aglow like tiny stars,
They gossip in bubbles, share sea's memoirs.
What tales they tell with such a flair,
Of lost flip-flops and turtle's hair!

In the stillness, they giggle and tease,
"Hey, watch me catch that floating breeze!"
With a clack and a snap, laughter rings true,
As they dance on the sands, beneath skies so blue.

The night carries jokes on currents that flow,
As crabs swap stories, putting on a show.
Whispers and chuckles, a night so bright,
In the depths of the ocean, all feels just right.

## Journeys on a Salty Journey

In search of snacks, they roam the shore,
With sneaky eyes and legs for more.
Taking a stroll with a curious grin,
A little roundabout, they spin and spin.

With seagulls laughing high on the breeze,
These creatures glide with utmost ease.
"Follow me, friends, to the sandy feast!"
And off they go, crabby eyes released.

Through seaweed jungles and coral gates,
They navigate seas, oh how fate awaits!
Laughing and pinching, making their way,
Each little adventure brings more display.

At the end of the tales, they gather back,
With shells worn and chests filled, no lack.
Journeys on salt, with giggles and cheer,
Crabs shed their shells, no worries, no fear!

## Silent Stride on Sandy Floors

On beaches wide, they tiptoe slow,
With sideways steps, a funny show.
Each grain of sand, a dance of fate,
Their charming moves, we celebrate.

In bright sun's glare, they lose their way,
Twirling here, then there to play.
A sideways glance, a cheerful grin,
Who knew the shoreline held such kin?

As waves come in, they scuttle fast,
A comical race, from tide to cast.
With claws raised high, they seem to boast,
Masters of sand, we cheer and toast.

At dusk, they gather, plotting schemes,
Retreat to burrows, in our dreams.
A party of shells, adventures bold,
In their silent strides, laughter's gold.

**Crustacean Tales Unwound**

Once in a tide, a tale was spun,
Of crabs who thought they were the fun.
In moonlit nights, they'd sing and dance,
With wiggly moves that made us prance.

They held a feast, on seaweed plates,
With plankton pies and shrimp-filled fates.
The dancing critters, all around,
In crabby jubilee, joy was found.

But who would win the crown of shell?
The judging panel, a clam named Mel.
With a wiggle and a puffed-out chest,
The winner flopped, "I'm truly blessed!"

So tales unwind, their laughter plays,
In seaside bars, through sunny days.
Join in the fun, with crustacean friends,
With all our laughter, the joy never ends.

## **Murmurs of the Briny Depths**

In the salty waves, a rumor brews,
Of crabs who tell the silliest views.
With pincers clashing, they call each name,
In underwater games, all seek their fame.

The bass hum a tune, a tinny bop,
Gossip travels fast, just won't stop.
"Did you see Fred?" "What of his shell?"
"Oh, I heard he fell; oh what a swell!"

With bubbles bright, a dance of glee,
They twirl and whistle, oh can't you see?
In briny blue, comedy stays,
In every chomp, and every sway.

So dive in deep, where chuckles rise,
In every wave, a funny surprise.
These murmurs shared in the ocean's hall,
With crustaceans prancing—come one, come all!

**Patterns in the Saline Mist**

In salty air, cheeky crabs roam,
Leaving their marks, like artists' foam.
With every step, they strike a pose,
"Look at us dance!" the little ones doze.

The tide brings secrets, whispers of fun,
As patterns emerge, we watch them run.
In circles and zigzags, a masterpiece,
Crustacean art, only adds to the fleece.

Each wave that crashes, a playful laugh,
They plot and plan, on their sandy path.
In curious shapes, they play their part,
The ocean's jesters, with crafty art.

So here's to the crabs, those jesters of beach,
With every swish and scuttle, they teach.
In patterns of joy, they dance and sway,
In twilight's glow, let's laugh and play!

## Guardians of the Gritty Sands

Tiny warriors in shells so neat,
Bandy about on their little feet.
With pincers raised and a wobbly gait,
They scuttle 'round, never tempt fate.

From sandcastle towers, they plot and plan,
How to outsmart a strolling man.
With a glittering eye and a twitching claw,
They declare the beach is now their law.

A rambunctious dance on the salty floor,
They twist, they turn, and then explore.
Silly antics cause giggles near,
As sand flies up, oh dear, oh dear!

Lurking beneath where shadows creep,
They nap and munch before a leap.
In this chaotic, sandy band,
Every pinch is gold, every grain a grand.

## The Symphony of the Shore

Nature's musicians, with rhythmic flares,
Compose their tunes in sun-kissed layers.
Pincers tap to the ocean's beat,
A bizarre concert with horns and feet.

A bold soloist pokes out in the fray,
While a timid one hides till the close of day.
With laughter rising and waves that sway,
Even the sea gull joins in their play.

High tide brings a raucous crowd,
As they dance and jive, oh so loud!
The beach is alive with their quirky sound,
In this sandy opera, joy is found.

Ever so clever, they know their score,
Though none have asked for an encore.
With a final flourish, they wave goodbye,
Leaving salty echoes beneath the blue sky.

## Depths of Resilience

In rocky homes where the sun is shy,
Creatures plot with a glint in their eye.
Against the waves, they stand their ground,
As laughter and clumsy moments abound.

Small but mighty in every way,
They crab their way through night and day.
With a chuckle at the twinkling stars,
They challenge the moon with their silly bars.

Creep along with a curious glee,
Adventure calls from the depths of the sea.
With a dash and a dance, into troubles they leap,
Finding treasures where it's dark and deep.

Once a speck in the ocean's swirl,
Now they flaunt with a twirl and a whirl.
For every stumble, they've got a tale,
Of the grand delights where others might pale.

## **Ruins of the Forgotten Sea**

Amidst the ruins where treasures lay,
A crusty crew prepares for play.
With laughter loud and voices sweet,
They turn old ships into a sandy treat.

Each hollow hull, a fort to defend,
Clawing at sand, a fun little trend.
With crusty crowns of driftwood and fray,
They rule the beach in their own funny way.

A rickety dance on a rusted hull,
They giggle and nudge, demanding a lull.
Digging for laughs in the salty air,
Every crumb of fun is a gem they share.

So if you stumble on this merry band,
Join their antics, take a stand.
For in the chaos, joy erupts,
And the spirit of fun is well corrupt.

## Woven Stories of the Coastal Realm

On shores where grains of sand do play,
A creature dances, bold and gay.
With pincers waving, oh what a sight,
While waves giggle, in sheer delight.

They scuttle sideways, a wobbly trot,
In shells adorned with plans they've got.
With each swift dodge, they play tag with fate,
As gulls look down, forecasting a plate.

With a wink and a nudge, they sneak on by,
Exchanging jokes as they jump and fly.
A feisty band of the ocean's jest,
In this watery circus, they laugh with zest.

So next time you wander to sandy shores,
Keep an eye peeled for their playful roars.
For in every pinch and playful scuffle,
Lies a story spun, a silly shuffle.

## The Weight of Carapace

He strutted along, a suit of mail,
With armor that sparkled, telling a tale.
Yet with each step, he'd wobble and weave,
Making observers gasp, then giggle and grieve.

His friends would snicker, "Look at him now,
Wearing that weight! What a silly vow!"
Yet he seemed proud, marching straight,
While others cheered, "Oh, it's just fate!"

His shell might be heavy, a load to bear,
But he'd spin in circles without a care.
While some would frown, he'd puff up his chest,
Claiming, "Who needs lightness? I'm simply the best!"

With each little challenge, he'd chirp with glee,
"Being this grand isn't hard, can't you see?"
In the dance of the tides, he's the king of the parade,
A jester of the sea, a charade well-played.

**Beneath the Surface**

Beneath the waves where the sea thoughts creep,
Busy little critters are losing sleep.
A crab with a secret, how cute and sly,
Crafts underwater shenanigans, oh my!

He claims to hold treasure, that shiny fan,
But really it's just a rusty can!
He polishes it, with pride and a grin,
As his crew bursts out laughing, "Not again!"

With tricks up his claws and a smirk wide,
He plays hide and seek with the tide as his guide.
But watch for the puffer that giggles aloud,
For his plans might just end in a bubbly crowd.

So delve beneath where the mirth remains,
Dancing with seaweed, while humor reigns.
For every little pinch holds a chuckle so grand,
In this underwater world, humor's perfectly planned.

## Stories Unfold

In the tide pools, the stories begin,
With a cast of characters thick as thin skin.
An actor with crust, and a plot full of glee,
With slapstick antics beneath the sea.

Each scuttle is scripted, every swap is a punch,
They bicker and banter, and sneak in a munch.
With a flip and a flail, they leap to the shore,
Hitching rides on a wave, then plotting some more.

With tales of the ones who dared to survive,
With laughter contagious, we feel so alive.
From crabby conundrums to fishy debates,
The humor runs deep, and it always creates.

So grab your popcorn, settle in place,
For tales of the shallow hold quite the space.
As we chuckle and cheer, beneath the warm sun,
The ocean's great stage is endlessly fun!

## The Ocean's Iron Will

In depths where the currents swirl and twine,
With a wily grin, the crustaceans dine.
"Who's tougher," they boast, with nibbles and bites,
With iron wills, they sing out their fights!

They march in a row, on brittle terrain,
A force of the ocean, wearing their brain.
With pincers raised high, they rumble and rave,
Claiming their thrones in this blue, briny wave!

While they clash for fun, it's all in jest,
A royal court in a shell-clad fest.
Giggling, they rally, with cheers from the flocks,
As absence of armor becomes their paradox.

So here's to the fun with a twist and a whirl,
Where joy hides in shells and laughter's a pearl.
In the ocean's embrace, let the stories unwind,
In this world of whimsy, it's laughter we find!

www.ingramcontent.com/pod-product-compliance
Lightning Source LLC
Chambersburg PA
CBHW070319120526
44590CB00017B/2747